At Bat

At Bat

Poems by

Mel Glenn

Kelsay Books

Cover photograph byAdam Vilimek
(licensed through shutterstock)

ISBN: 978-1-947465-66-4

Kelsay Books
Aldrich Press
www.kelsaybooks.com

Dedicated to baseball fans everywhere...

Contents

End Poems

About the Author

Introduction

Sports and Michelangelo

The seasons come and go,
speaking of Michelangelo,
and as the heat gathers,
sports capture the only true constant.
In summer, there's baseball,
In winter, football and basketball.
Team fortunes rise and fall,
as do my emotions when I follow
my Mets, Knicks and Giants.
I place myself on the field;
my own trials seem trivial.
Sports have always been my haven,
something mine, something to embrace.
I once dreamed of becoming a sportswriter,
but it proved too competitive for my timid soul.
But now sports are my refuge, my place on the couch,
providing warmth and light from the TV screen.
I wonder if Michelangelo ever kicked a ball around.

A Baseball/Poetry Link?

When my team is playing good ball,
words flow from my pen
as clean as a line single to right.
My metaphors take flight and fall
in the reader's lap out in the bleachers.
Inspiration comes to me,
as brilliant as a manager's hunch
to go with the hit and run.
But when my team has lost five in a row,
my words seem frozen in the batter's box,
much like a batter fooled by a called third strike.
My metaphors never bounce past the pitcher's mound,
and my similes prompt the crowd
to roundly boo my creative efforts.
Inspiration fails me,
as deflating as a final 11-0 drubbing.
So, Mr. Manager, get your team to do better.
Then maybe my literary work will be a hit.

Poetry in the Minor Leagues

Sitting on the bench, waiting
for my doubtful turn at bat,
I stare out across the old ball field
at the old manufacturing plant,
just beyond the right field fence.
It used to turn out poems,
supplying a living wage
to writers and poets of all ages.
They would have worked for nothing, you know,
enjoying the sunrises and sunsets over the river,
describing various colors of the sky's palette.
With paper and pen, they carved out
intricate and masterful work,
but now all writing has been
transferred to the city, pulsing
electronically from place to place,
often without any artistic input at all.
The factory and the ball park closed ten years ago,
and my call up to the majors
now seems doubtful at best.

The Poems

A Cup of Coffee

When I was called up late last September,
the crowd heard my name over the PA,
before I pitched an inning of relief.
I gave up two hits, but no runs scored.
Soon after, they released me, saying
I wasn't in "their long-range plans."
I went back to Texas to watch my parents grow old.
I'd quit baseball if there was anything I love as much.
Got lucky as another club invited me to spring training.
So, here I am, now on the flip side of 30,
having spent my twenties climbing the baseball ladder
with a pitching arm that is not as strong as before.
I don't know if I can do this anymore;
maybe I'll just go back home.
But I was a major leaguer once,
if only for one inning,
if only for a sip, not a whole cup of coffee.
I guess no one will hear my name now.

A Singles Hitter

I'm standing on first base,
courtesy of a walk, a free pass,
and really do not have the personality
to take the risk to try and steal second.
I have been playing this game for years,
and have to admit I am strictly a singles hitter,
one who has managed upon occasion
to hit the ball past the drawn-in infielders.
People in the stands begin to yawn
as I take a very short lead off the bag.
The next batter, perhaps seeing my cautious life,
gives me an opportunity to run by taking
a couple of pitches, but I stay put.
He strikes out and I return to right field,
hoping that no one will hit the ball to me.
I am safe for now, yet sometimes I wonder
how it would feel to round second, head for third,
and come flying home as the crowd goes crazy.

A Visit to The Therapist

A baseball player visits his therapist
during the off-season
"Doc, you gotta help me.
I had a lousy season, only batted .247,
and I want to know why.
My lack of hits, were they due to
trauma caused by my father beating my mother?
Were my errors a product of low self-esteem,
given that my father rarely complimented me?
Did my rivalry with my brother cause me
to be overly aggressive at the plate?
Is my failure with women
a result of years spent in the company of men?
And finally, my need to chew tobacco?
Because I wasn't breast-fed as an infant?
In my dreams I run around in circles,
instead of round the diamond.
Doc, can you help me have a better year?"
His therapist: "Now we will begin."

Another Openin' Another Show

If baseball were a Broadway play
no doubt there would be a drama with
a walk-off homer ringing down the curtain.
Or maybe it would morph into a comedy
full of blunders and missed chances
but I say baseball owes its roots to the
distinctly American art form—the musical
To wit, some songs:
"Some Enchanted Evening"—
the first night game under the stars
"Tradition"—speaks for my loyalty as I
have suffered through countless seasons
"Wouldn't It Be Loverly"—if my team
could actually win a series
"Sixteen Going on Seventeen"—a really
long extra-innings game
"My Favorite Things"—what could be better
than a hot dog and some beer?
"Climb Every Mountain "—my woebegone
team after losing five straight games
"Shall We Dance?"—the runner leads off first
"You'll Never Walk Alone" the—pitcher
just put three men on base
"If I Were a Rich Man"—I'd buy a season's ticket
"Send in the Clowns"—the bull pen's kinda weak
And finally,
"I Dreamed a Dream"—that my team will play
in the World Series
Happy Opening Day

As If Written In 1908

Go you beloved Metropolitans,
you mighty men who smote
the hapless denizens of Chicago,
a valiant, if inexperienced
aggregation of formidable batsmen,
hitless wonders who tried their best,
their best not good enough
to withstand the furious onslaught
of the vaunted twirlers of Gotham
who hurled their heavenly orbs
against the bats that futilely fanned
the Indian summer air.
So onward Murphy, Cespedes and Wright.
Forge a plethora of four-baggers.
Onward Harvey, Syndergaard, DeGrom.
Battle the American League opposition
with your incandescent deliveries.
Nothing but World Series glory
and joyful hosannas
await your prodigious production
guaranteeing certain victory.

Ballet of Baseball

It's a dance, you know.
Consider just one play:
Batter hits ground ball towards second.
He runs along the base path.
The second baseman bends
to catch the ball.
The first baseman skips towards the bag,
lifts his glove ready to catch the throw.
He stretches, reaching to keep
one foot on the base.
The runner pumps his legs to beat the throw.
The ball and the runner arrive at the same time.
The umpire yells, "Safe!"
Just a few seconds have past,
but this brief ballet has excited the crowd –
the last out!
Pitcher and catcher leave the field entwined.
The dance will be repeated tomorrow,
indeed repeated all summer long.

Ballplayer's Lament

"I've lost 5 mph on my fastball."
There are millions starving in Africa
"I went 0-4 today."
Italian town buried by volcanic eruption
"What a dumb-ass base running mistake."
They just hijacked a tanker off Somalia
"I think they're gonna send me down to Triple A."
North Korea fired four missiles
"I don't wanna go to the bullpen."
A quarter of Antarctica has drifted away
"I hate playin' in this town."
Congress questions ties to Russia
Pre-season rants, locker room complaints,
(why won't the press leave me alone?)
All utterances spoken by heroes,
our men in boys' clothing, sounding off
as the world spins towards the apocalypse.
But let's play ball, shall we?
That's the only thing that's really important.

Baseball as Extended Metaphor II

As a kid, you were told by parents and coaches
to follow the rules, stay within the lines,
run consecutively to first, second, and then third,
be alert to catch what life throws at you.
But there is no crying in baseball or life;
you must accept the verities of the game.
But what if you wanted to run when you liked,
frolic happily from third to second to first,
dance out of boredom in the outfield,
come up to the plate when it's not your turn,
thus violating the printed lineup
of a most ordered, regimented life?
What if you wanted to play more than
nine innings, with the score untied?
What if you wanted to play in the rain,
or not play at all because you didn't feel like it?
Then what would the umpire and all
the authoritarian arbiters we live by
say then?

Baseball, Southern Style

Here in the Deep South,
not too far from the Everglades,
heat and humidity hang like a curtain
over the partially-filled stadium.
Everything seems to take longer—
the time between pitches,
the exchange of places after three outs,
the walk to the concession stand for hot dogs and beer.
The fastest people around are the local kids
who scamper from dugout to dugout
for a souvenir ball tossed to them from a good-hearted player
coming off the field after the third out.
Even when the ball is in play,
the pursing fielders seem to move in molasses,
reflecting the game's pastoral and leisurely roots.
So small is the crowd that individual voices
can be heard urging the Class A team to "Let's Go!"
And when the game finally oozes to an end,
both fans and players exit with languid grace,
with nothing better to do
until the slow moving clock of baseball
ticks at its own pace, unhurriedly,
to begin another game under a sweltering sky.

Baseball's Pace

Baseball's pace matches my own,
a leisurely walk to first base,
from where I can survey
the vast field of my life,
from where I can reflect on
the blue of the sky,
and the green of the grass.
There's no hurry at my age,
more time to watch the stillness of the pitcher
before he fires his fastball towards home,
more time to watch the batter at the plate
as he digs into his boxed life, making adjustments,
trying to launch the ball and his career,
and finally, more time to enjoy the kids
who, with innocence, look up to their heroes.
There's no need for me to steal second,
to hurry up and round the bases.
There's plenty of need, though,
to stand still for the moment, take it all in,
and revel in the pleasures of the game.

Benita Alvarez

My Papa says he loves us all the same,
but I do not want one quarter of his love,
just because I have three other sisters,
who, if you ask me, are always silly.
They chase boys and dress in such ways
my Momma refuses to let them out of the house.
Papa, I am going to be better than my sisters.
I am going to be better than any boy.
Watch me lift weights, do sprints,
and when spring comes, I will try out
for our school's championship softball team.
You'll see, I'll make you proud of me.
What—you want me to play shortstop?
No problemo—watch me throw a frozen rope to first.
Papa, I'll play any position you want.
Papa says he loves us all the same.
This is not true; my Papa will love me more.

Billy Shakespeare Waiting For Spring Training

When in disgrace and with no fortune in men's eyes,
I all alone beweep my outcast state,
And trouble deaf heavens with, "Where is my baseball?"
And look upon myself and curse my fate,
Wishing me like to one more rich in hope,
Looking like him with friends possessed,
Desiring that ballplayer's skill with bat and glove,
With what I most enjoy contented least;
Yet in these thoughts myself almost despising,
Haply, I think on thee, oh, baseball, and then my mood
(Like a lark at the break of day arising
From sullen earth) I sing hymns at heaven's gate;
For my sweet love of the game such wealth brings,
That then I scorn to change my state with kings.

Coney Island Ball

Once there were three great amusement parks
that twisted, raised, dropped people in dizzying degree.
The Wonder Wheel is a wind-blown spider's web,
the Parachute Jump, a discarded animal's skeleton,
and in the shadow of the one remaining coaster,
the landmarked Cyclone, there is a ball park here,
nestled against the ocean, open to Friday night fireworks.
Dreams begin anew each year here in Class A ball,
each player hoping he will make it to the big show.
Little kids line up at the fence, waiting
to get autographs of future major leaguers.
Dreams end here, too, as injuries crop up,
as unwanted as weeds in the outfield grass.
The home team catcher goes 4 for 4 this night,
believing, for the moment, his performance
has earned him a ticket upwards, at least to Double A.
The minor league park shudders at such hubris.
There is a ball park here, you know,
a silent crossing guard, noting
the passage of young men going up and down.
It's a short, short, season, boys, so swing away.
The gold ring is yours for the taking.

Danny Vargas

My father drinks, so I don't stay home much.
My teachers bore me, so I don't go to class much.
Baseball is my life, my present, my future.
When I take the relay from Conti
and cut down the runner trying to score from first,
there's no thrill in the world that comes close.
Not even sex.
I have to scratch for everything,
beating our grounders,
dodging inside pitches,
advancing the runner over to third.
I thought I was doin' fine
until coach threw me a nasty curve
that sent me sprawling to the dirt.
He said I couldn't play no more because
I had failed three subjects.
He asked me to turn in my uniform.
I refused and ran out of his office, crying,
onto the field, to the batter's box,
to the only place I can call home.

Die-Hard Fan

Is it possible to die easy
and still be a fan?
Or must your demise
occur in some spectacular way
to prove your abiding loyalty?
Then there is this to consider:
If you are quite dead,
and buried deep in the ground,
how can you still be a fan?
Wave a pennant from the crypt?
Cheer from the edge of the cemetery?
It is difficult enough these days
to be a live-hard fan, living as I do
in the midst of a losing streak
suffered by my beloved New York Mets.
I don't know how much more I can endure.
The team is sending me to an early grave,
where I will be fully justified
in calling myself a true "Die-Hard Fan."

Emily Knew Baseball

Research just turned up has indicated
Emily certainly knew her baseball,
and were she alive today,
this New Englander would be a Red Sox fan.
To wit:
"Hope is the thing with feathers."
Obviously, she is talking about spring training,
where every team in a potential pennant contender.
"People need hard times…to develop psychic muscles."
Manager says I know last year was rough.
"If I can stop one heart from breaking,
I shall not live in vain."
Manager says that this year will be better.
"Luck is not chance; it's toil."
Manager says we'll work hard, give 110% every game.
"Saying nothing sometimes says the most."
Manager says he's through talking,
will let his players just play ball.
So, in the springtime of our hopes,
dear Emily, say a prayer for our team,
our poor, woebegone, but beloved team.

Fathers and Sons

The son wanted to take his father to a ball game,
not that he loved baseball all that much,
but realized on some inarticulate level
time was running out on a better relationship
with the man he didn't know all that well.
The son planned the day with care—
good seats, what topics to cover.
To be sure, there were some subjects to avoid,
like his father's criticism of his choice of a career,
his father's distance from the son's new wife.
(Wasn't he always kind of distant?)
But troubling questions faded in the
resplendent light of a cheering stadium.
The food was delicious; the home team even won.
The currency of the language was the game itself.
"Why didn't they bunt then?'
"When will they bring in a new pitcher?"
The son was surprised how much baseball his father knew.
On the trip home he thought it a good day,
but realized with a start, he and his father
were no closer now, but then again,
they weren't further apart either.

Field of Dreams

I used to think baseball was too slow for me
as I dashed through my 30s, 40s, and 50s,
tending to life's changes of speed,
but now that I'm in my 60s, baseball's pace
seems to more closely match my own rhythm.
I take a keener interest in
a southpaw's looping, inviting curve,
or the emergence of this year's batting champ.
This year I looked at the standings in both leagues,
and noticed how many games my beloved Mets were behind.
I attended games now and then and caught my breath
when the green fields opened up before me.
I checked the out-of-town scoreboard
and felt sorry for the teams sixteen games out.
Baseball has brought me back home,
back to the playing field of my childhood,
to the time when my Ebbets Field heroes
strode like giants along the base paths,
and when I hoped against hope my father
would stop working and play catch with me.

Game Called on Account Of....

"Here we are, ladies and gentlemen,
in Cleveland or Chicago (doesn't matter),
where the game time temperature is 27,
and a moderate snowstorm is coming in from the lake.
The faithful clap their thunder sticks
in an effort to keep warm.
Chicago's leadoff batter has a shovel in his hands,
ready for the pitch as the Cleveland hurler
starts his windup intent on directing
his first snowball towards the strike zone.
His catcher seems to have some trouble
putting down the signs because his fingers have frozen.
Crack of the shovel and there is a snowball liner
heading deep to the outfield whereupon it
explodes with a splat in the left fielder's glove.
Time for the relief pitcher to be called in.
He opens the fence, climbs on his snowmobile,
and heads for the mound, windshield wipers
activated on his sunglasses, also to ward off the glare.
Then sanity prevails as the umpires gather in their parkas
and mercifully call the game on account of ice."

Girls and Baseball

You can only fall in love once
for the first time,
with a girl, with your team.
You remember when the attraction was new,
the sweep of her hair,
the sweep of the field,
the grace when she walked,
the grace when they hit,
the beauty of her winning ways,
the beauty of their winning ways.
They both broke your heart, you know,
when she moved to the Midwest,
when they moved to the coast.
You never forget your first loves;
pictures of both stay in your head.
Though new teams and new girls
reappear with promise each spring,
you remain loyal and secretly wish
they would both come back to you,
declaring anew first loves prove indelible,
no matter the time, no matter the season.

Grapefruit League

On this sun-drenched Florida field,
nobody has booted a grounder,
and nobody has thrown a ball away.
Nobody has taken a called third strike,
and nobody has missed a signal.
There's excitement in the stands,
as retirees dream of past championships,
or, at least, a remembered run at the playoffs.
"We will win at least 90 games," the manager promises.
"Our pitching is that good and we have
a veteran corps of players to support our youngsters."
This is the best time,
when dreams float across the sky,
as lazily as pop flies,
and hope is as happy as
a safe call at third base.
This is the best time, a kid's playground,
before the reality of the first fastball
comes sizzling across home plate.

Happy Girl at The Ballpark

At Citi Field here in New York,
I held the swing door open for her,
and she thanked me with a smile.
I wish I had the verbal camera acuity
to capture the totality of that girl.
Desperate to hold on to her image,
I penned a quick biography—
Her name is Sarah, newly arrived from Nashville.
She is an actress, of course, or wishes to be,
and an avid fan of the Nashville Sounds,
the Triple A farm team of the Brewers.
When Sarah speaks, her words
as slow as a lazy change, invite you in,
to sit with her on the front porch at home,
or maybe accompany her to Greer Stadium
to watch her beloved team play.
I had no camera, tape or video
to capture that ball park freeze frame,
and even if I did, I realize my small art
would be, at best, a mere approximation.
I may have watched my Mets flail for nine innings,
but all I remember of that day is Sarah's smile.

He Never Heard of Bobby Thompson

The hipster at Starbucks
looked over his computer
and stared at my Mets cap.
"They might make it this year," he said,
which led to a discussion
of famous baseball collapses.
"The most brutal one
was Bobby Thompson's home run," I said.
"Who's that?" he asked.
What? How could he not know?
He listened while I described
the ruination of my childhood
when Russ Hodges screamed
over the airwaves into my bedroom
"The Giants win the pennant!
The Giants win the pennant!"
For the moment I felt so terribly old,
like some prehistoric baseball dinosaur.
The hipster promised to google
the 1951 Dodger/Giants series.
The ghosts of my beloved bums—
Branca, Newcombe, Labine, et al
whispered their thanks to me
from across the span of years.

Hot Stove League

As any baseball fan knows,
when snow covers the diamond,
and the northern winds chill our bones,
the only recourse we have is to sit,
metaphorically, beside a pot-bellied stove
and offer suggestions on how best
to improve our favorite put-upon teams.
Please, Mr. G.M., can you cook me up
a flavorful recipe for a winning season?
Can you stir the pot
and let the cream of players
rise to the surface?
Can you light a match under your manager?
Can you bake me a clutch batter,
saute a seasoned shortstop,
fry a five-tool right fielder,
and roast me a quality reliever,
without fear of making a wrong cut?
I just need an alphabet soup bowl of hope
as I wait for the warmth and promise
of spring training to return.

If Langston Hughes Played Baseball

I've known baseball;
I've known baseball as
ancient as the centuries
and older than the flow of
pitch and catch across the generations.
My soul has grown deep like baseball.
I bathed in the early morning light
when the sun dawned over the right field fence,
and built my house near Ebbets Field,
as the pastoral game lulled me to sleep.
I looked upon the ball parks and raised
the mound in the middle of the diamond.
I heard the singing of fastballs
when Walter "Big Train" Johnson
came east from semi-pro ball in Idaho.
I have seen the muddy fields prior to a rain-out.
I've known baseball:
ancient, dusky double-headers.
My soul has grown deep like baseball.

In Praise of The Long-Relief Man

Most of us are not baseball stars.
In fact, we hardly approach fame
in our normal, humdrum lives.
We work, pay mortgages, raise kids,
without even the hint of any applause.
We slog through our days in near silence,
in near obscurity, in near anonymity.
The only one who truly understands
is the indefatigable long-relief pitcher
who puts in his time and effort
so responsibly, so unobtrusively
that everyone can eventually go home
to down a beer or two.
He punches his innings with resignation,
much like the factory worker who
day after day resolutely clocks in and out.
Both are to be honored for their fortitude;
both keep the gears turning—
in the game, in life,
both unrecognized by those
who remember neither
their names or numbers.

In Praise of The Lowly Bunt

Oh, ye of little distance,
the favored stroke of players and pitchers
mired below the Mendoza line,
square up your shoulders,
and your bat, stand with pride
that your dribble down the line
weighs more important than
a towering fly ball out.
What greater call than to sacrifice,
to lay down your life to advance the runner.
You may never be heralded
on the evening sports broadcasts,
nor achieve acclaim within
the halls of Cooperstown.
But true aficionados of the game know
the importance of your achievements
has little to do with length.
So, continue your shortened travels
along the infield grass, confident
it is not necessarily a bad thing
to come up a little bit short.

Major League Error

A simple ground ball of an obligation,
a slow roller of a promise
to show up on time at hallowed ground
to bear witness for the man who died at home,
and I muffed it!
The manager was forced to find another player
to go out onto the field for me,
someone who could stand up at the plate
and say *Kaddish* for the dead.
I will never play for the angels,
upper or lower case,
and my soul will suffer on the injured reserve list.
But maybe the Ultimate Commissioner
might grant me another chance tomorrow
to suit up for my religion, take an at bat
to sing for all those who have played
many championship seasons in leagues
of both major and minor consequences.
They are all to be honored,
this side of Cooperstown.

Metrics Shmetrics

It's the time of the year
when baseball experts
come out of the woodwork,
dust off their crystal balls,
and pontificate on
what teams will place where.
They dutifully consult all kinds of metrics
to forecast winners and losers in each division.
But the Gods of Baseball mischievously
have other plans in mind.
They decide who gets hurt,
who has a hot streak,
who has punched his ticket to the show.
How fruitless it is to predict
who will win, who will lose,
who will make the play
that will change the course of one's life.
Ah, the vagaries, the unknowns
that make it impossible to forecast
the bounces in baseball, the bounces in life.

Missing Baseball

As winter clutches me by the throat,
with snow beginning to fall,
(though not as bad as my upstate neighbors
who must shovel snow off their roofs,)
I dream of green fields and worn gloves,
and hot afternoons of sandlot games,
where childhood stretches out forever.
Basketball's too fast, football too violent,
and only the tradition of pitch and catch
matches the peaceful feelings I seek.
Come ye heroes of my past,
emerge from your icy caverns,
and cavort on the field of my imagination.
Me, at the plate, spraying balls to left, center and right.
Me, at first, completing the DP with a nice scoop.
Me, in the bleachers with hot dog and soda,
losing all track of time,
until I am urged to drop my reverie,
button up my coat, and do a little
pre-Thanksgiving shoveling of my own.

My Father Did Not Play

Unlike "Field of Dreams,"
my father did not play catch with me.
Indeed, he did not know
a football from a baseball,
but taught me instead the pitch of language.
I learned how to be my father's son,
my singles, new words,
my home runs, well-constructed paragraphs.
As I turned to manhood,
rounded the bases of my career,
I even fielded a family of my own.
I did not teach my own sons
the finer points of pitch and catch,
but instructed them instead
on the virtues of a greater vocabulary.
The result of this education,
means one less person in the stands,
and one less story of a father
playing catch with his son,
something lost then, a pastime in peril.

My Mother Took Me to The Ball Game

Such shame!
My mother took me to Ebbets Field,
home of the old Brooklyn Dodgers.
There was no greater embarrassment
than being escorted by my mother.
(Wasn't that something a dad was supposed to do?)
Neither parent knew the difference
between a football and a baseball,
having spent years in Europe.
I was only hoping that none of my
sixth-grade classmates would see me there.
My mother, though, was quite content
to do her needlework, hardly looking at the field,
while I peeked out from under my jacket
to watch my beloved heroes
in their blue and white uniforms.
I was horrified that my secret would be revealed,
and subsequently mocked the next day in school.
I bobbed between fear and joy.
Only years later did I realize
my mother's love in taking me,
far outweighed any shame I felt then.

Not Ready to Call the Game

Baseball – the language between fathers and sons,
familiar terms of runs and relief pitchers
and second-guessing the manager's decision.
"Did you see the game last night?" I email,
code for how come you don't call me often enough.
"You think the team will be better than .500?"—
subterfuge for why don't you tell me
what's really on your (home) plate these days?
I know you're swinging for the financial fences these days,
and the economy is as shaky as the old ball park,
but I am stranded far away from the action on your field.
So let me into the game once in a while.
Toss a conversational ball up to me in the stands.
Explain to me your preparation for facing the competition
while we sit with our hot dogs and beer.
I am not ready to call it a game yet,
and drift back to the cornfields of dotage.
I am standing at the plate now, awaiting your pitch
to re-establish after a long (rain) delay
the fastball connections between fathers and sons.

Now Batting, #4, The Poet

Can a poet make a living,
chasing lines instead of line drives?
Can he make contact with a hot metaphor
or loft a deep poem into the 4th stanza seats?
Can he bat .1000 with his editor and
push forward a haiku down the third base line?
Meanwhile, the pitcher/poet warms up his writing arm
at his desk in the bullpen in anticipation of coming in,
and slamming a verse right down the middle.
The crowd anxiously awaits his first appearance in print,
chanting, "Let's go poet, let's go poet."
The batter/poet steps out of the box,
sharpens his pencils, checks his email.
Then he goes back to work,
spraying his words to all corners of the field.
After the game, young acolytes
gather at the fence to ask for autographs,
waiting for the day when they, too,
will have their chance to hit the long ball poem.

Obit: Charlie Williams

A common enough name,
he died in surgery, age 67.
Once, he was a ballplayer
for the early New York Mets.
He wasn't a star;
he never made a lot of money,
but he had one claim to fame.
He was the player traded to the Giants
to get the legendary, but fading, Willie Mays.
Imagine your whole life summed up
in a small obit in the back pages.
What's your value?
Bait in a baseball trade?
A commodity to be dangled?
Afterwards, Charlie left baseball,
drove a cab, drifted a bit,
never to be heard from again.
Hold your sympathy, fans.
He may be a footnote in agate type,
but he was a major league ballplayer.
How many of us can say that?

On Hearing the Learned Baseball Man*

Years ago, when I heard the learned baseball man
speak of averages, pitch counts, and the
durability of his team's core of relievers,
when his proofs and figures
were arranged in columns before him,
when I saw the charts, diagrams,
how soon, unaccountable, I became tired and sick,
til rising and gliding out, I wandered off by myself,
and walked out to the mound of
my son's Little League ball field.
Baseball's very slow moving, I thought,
and maybe I can keep him 10 forever.
Both sons have moved to other fields of interest,
and I, I, wish now there was a new ball park in the moonlight
I could visit at age 70, today, in fact,
stop time and watch my son waiting for his pitch.

* Apologies to Whitman

On Losing

When my team has lost four in a row,
why do I acutely feel the pain?
When my team has been shut out once again,
why must I play the part of a shut-in,
refusing to go out into the sunlight?
When my favorite ballplayer goes 0 for 4,
why do I feel I might be sent down to Triple-A?
I cannot control the tides.
I cannot control the wind.
I have little influence over
what friends and family are wont to do.
There is preciously little of my fate I am master of.
Shouldn't I receive some sad solace
for my longtime loyalty?
Shouldn't my years of dumb allegiance
be rewarded by a victory now and then?
C'mon guys, scratch out a win.
I can't afford to wait 'til next year.
My life is running out of seasons.

On Taking His Girlfriend to A Ballgame

On their third date, he wanted
to impress her with his generosity.
He brought her flowers and presented her with a box
containing two front row seats along the 1st base line.
She thought it would be jewelry.
"Have you ever seen a ball game?" he asked.
"On TV."
"No, I mean live."
"Nope."
"You'll love it, trust me."
At the ballpark she commented on
the green of the grass, the blue of the sky.
"Oh, look at the 1st baseman, he's cute," she observed.
"He's batting .223."
"I like him anyway."
She spent the game eating corn dogs, downing beers
and watching other people in the stands.
"Did you like the game?" he asked afterwards.
"It was fun," she said.
He knew it was the start of a beautiful relationship.

On the Radio

I miss baseball games on radio,
listening on my portable set
to the silken Southern drawl of Red Barber.
I didn't need an 80 inch screen,
instant replay and too young announcers
who over-broadcast games today.
Then, I could imagine parks
in Chicago, St. Louis and Pittsburgh,
while reading comics under the covers
as the game hovered all around me.
Baseball, they say now is much too slow,
but it was fast enough for me.
My heroes could remain heroes
without the public spectacle of
crotch-grabbing, spitting, and
other off-the-field steroid stories.
Even the beer commercials were fun then.

Opening Day

Before the first error, the first strikeout,
it is possible to dream of
winning streaks, walk-off home runs,
and the wind that carries your hopes
as high as an arcing blast that settles
deep into the right field bleachers.
I am nine,
and the little league field lays out before me;
I am sixty-nine,
and my heart lays out on the green carpet,
as ballplayers, young enough to be my grandsons,
take the field on opening day.
I am in the ball park, the box seats, with beer,
yelling for my beloved home team.
I am on the mound in my mind,
peering in for the catcher's sign.
What? He walked on four pitches?
No matter, get the next batter.
Time, past, present, and future,
presented to me by the baseball gods,
who have granted me one more season in the sun.

Opening Day II

"Hope may be the thing with feathers,"
Emily Dickinson said, but it's clear
she never attended an opening day game.
Forget about feathers, my dear Emily.
Hope is the smell of the ballpark,
under a crystal-blue sky.
Hope is the speed of the first pitch thrown,
which is called for a strike.
Hope is the first long fly ball
that has a chance of going yard.
No thought of a losing game or season now.
Emily, if you were alive today,
I'd take you to opening day.
We'd have good seats in the reserved section.
I'd buy you a hot dog, and if
you were still hungry, a pretzel as well.
And when my home team wins,
as assuredly it must,
then you would know what hope truly is.

Pitch and Catch

My son and I speak
the coded language of baseball.
"They should wait 'til next year."
"They have no pitching."
"They should bring up their entire Triple A team."
—all general observations that cover like a tarp
the lack of real pitch and catch between us.
Apparently, something there is
that doesn't like an (outfield) wall
as we toss soft balls to each other
in ritualistic pregame warmups.
We observe the rules,
the polite formalities of the game,
but hide our true feelings,
much like the catcher who shields
his signals from the opposing team.
This late in the season,
sitting in opposite dugouts,
it's hard to accept
we are not playing on the same side.

Pitch Perfect #1

Baseball metaphors come easily
as I stand at the poetic plate
on this opening day of the season.
I wave my pen, ready to swing away,
ready to bounce my words off the left field wall.
But first, I have to dig in, concentrate,
and focus my vision on my field of dreams.
Thwack!—an image flies off my bat, a first hit,
and then a rally of nouns, adjectives and verbs.
I am in the zone now, watch out, as I
spray ideas into left, center and right.
In other plate appearances,
I may send a soft line to left,
bloop a double entendre to right,
or float a simile out to center.
Maybe with enough times at bat,
I'll become the MVP—Most Valuable Poet.
With enough swings I can hope to hit
a poem out of the park.

Pitch Perfect #2

Sometimes, it's not about metaphors at all.
Sometimes, it's just about baseball,
the smell of the field, the swing of the bat,
the sandlot games I played
when I was 12 and guarded the first base line.
We were the Generals then, and I was #14,
in honor of my hero, Gil Hodges.
We didn't have uniforms, just tee-shirts,
and Bobby Tzchechik was our shortstop and captain.
No hovering parents, no Little League rules,
just boys tossing the ball around,
before the game became a business,
as the sun went down on our childhood.
I looked for my old glove the other day,
but it got traded for credit cards and mortgage payments,
thereby becoming a metaphor once again.

Pitchers and Catchers

C'mon, Old Man Winter,
hit me with your best shot.
I am not afraid of you.
Bring on your Buffalo blizzards,
your icy polar vortex.
Pile snow upon my doorstep,
and let the plows bury my car.
Frosty, the Snowman and Jack Frost
can gang up and pelt me with snowballs.
I am perfectly content to wait you out,
to stay inside my nice house,
and stand next to the radiator
with a cup of hot tea warming my hands.
I will amuse myself by watching
your antics on the Weather Channel.
Do blankets of your winter whiteness
depress me? Not in the least.
Pitchers and catchers report
in just a couple of weeks.

Poet/Ballplayer

*Note: Adrian Cardenas, who played 45 games for the Chicago Cubs in 2012,
now is studying writing and philosophy at NYU.*
—from The New York Times, 8/9/14

"You wouldn't think so, but there are a lot
of similarities between baseball and writing,
the most obvious of which is,
both crafts contain the seeds of failure.
A .200 hitter has failed to reach base 80% of the time,
and as any editor will tell you, the odds of
acceptance for a manuscript is under one percent.
But a beautiful line of poetry seems like a towering fly,
a perfect metaphor, as thrilling as a no-hit game,
an exact rhyme, the crack of the bat,
drafts and rewrites, time in the batting cage,
and the completion of a poem, the big W.
Few poets can express the lyricism
of a green outfield on a Sunday afternoon.
Yet, despite the beauty of the game,
I chose the pen over the bat.
A ballplayer lives for a season;
a poet lives for eternity."

Radio Days

Then,
the broadcasted games
played the Muzak of our lives.
A transistor radio blared,
while we ran through stoop ball,
off-the-curb, and, of course, baseball.
We imagined there were little ballplayers
playing on little fields inside our radios.
Now,
we as pot-belied old men
sitting on our lawn chairs
in the Florida shade
listen again to the radio,
not as background,
but as highlight of the day.
We,
don't hear the present hurried announcers,
but the old Southern gentlemen
who spoke as if each word, and each play,
were to be savored over the long, hot afternoon.

Rooting for A .500 Team

It's like walking up the down staircase.
It's like flipping a coin, heads or tails.
It's like living in the calm center
between wild elation and deep despair.
It's like hitching your wagon to a star,
and watching it slog along within the speed limit.
I do not want a middle-of-the-road life.
I want my fandom on the precipice of passion,
with winning or losing not mattering much,
(though winning is probably better).
I want to scream with delight
at the appearance of a winning streak.
I want to wail in misery
at the appearance of a losing one.
I will not be lulled into
the ordinariness of a routine pop fly.
Come on guys,
choose one direction or the other.
Let me feel alive again.

Rooting for A Losing Team

Baseball is a cosmic game of Chutes and Ladders.
Year after year I find myself
at the bottom of the slide,
my legs splayed, my stomach churned,
sitting in a heap, wondering,
if in my lifetime, I'll ever climb to the top.
Once, twenty-seven years ago,
my Mets defeated the Red Sox Nation,
but since then it's been a Biblical drought,
a Dust Bowl of dried up dreams
with the realization there is
nothing growing down on the farm.
I can only watch the current crop,
and writhe in exquisite agony
with my only stalk of hope—
believing next year will bear better fruit.
Rooting for a losing team actually fortifies me,
in that I am not quite alone in living
the descending arc of my life.

Rout

What does the losing right fielder think of
in the middle of a 12-1 rout?
It must be hard to concentrate on the game.
Does he entertain the possibility of a comeback?
Does he think about a to-do list?
Does he wonder about what he will eat for dinner?
Or maybe he's more philosophical.
It's only one game, right?
What will I do after baseball?
Wasn't that woman I met last night cute?
I imagine myself out in right field,
whatever the score.
I am a major leaguer—who knew?
I am making big bucks.
I don't care if I ever see a fly ball.
Truth is, we will never know what is on his mind,
a memory, a sudden insight, a song, perhaps.
But for now, for us, he is just a stick figure
out in right field, stuck in the mire of a lost game.

Scouting Report

"Though he may well be a
promising minor league poet,
probably of Triple A caliber,
We doubt he is ready for the Big Show now.
He can certainly field all kinds of topics,
albeit with limited vision, but his poetic swing
demonstrates a lack of bat speed and consistency.
He is rather rigid in his poetic stance,
and is not amenable to changing his grip on
unrhymed free verse of 15-20 lines.
He has not shown the kind of power
necessary to clear the literary fences.
His poetry, while unsuited to
the pastoral demands of the game,
nevertheless does exhibit an urban uniqueness.
What we like best about him is
his gritty tenacity over 1300 poems.
We wish him well, but at this point in time,
cannot see offering him a Major League contract."

Small Town Ball

Major, even minor league dreams long gone,
these weathered men in their 30s,
already beer-bellied and balding,
gathered at the local ball field Sunday
for their grudge match against the younger men
from FoundryWorks, next town over.
The older men tried to will their minds
to the speed and memories of their youth.
Discarding minor injuries,
the home team threw themselves
into the passions of the game,
bragging rights more important than
the $50 side wager per man.
The ensuing 8-0 rout depressed them more than
the money pocketed by the away team.
The locals trudged home with a new set of aches.
They didn't tell their wives about the money,
but the women knew anyway, said nothing,
realizing it would do no good
to deprive their husbands of their pride,
a small price to pay for evening peace.

Snow - Field of Dreams

The city has been buried under 28 inches of snow.
    I'm thinking about baseball.
My car lies buried by a snow plow.
    I dream of green fields and batting gloves.
There's no food left in my frig.
    I salivate over hot dogs and beer.
I stumble in the slush.
    I want to slide into second.
In the winter of my discontent,
I yearn for the boys of summer.
Yes, give me
no more snowballs, but fast balls,
no more winter hats, but baseball caps,
no *El Niño*, but the Bambino.
More snow? No Thanks,
Bring on the New York Yanks.
No more winter's whitish view,
honestly, I'd rather play two.

Sports Injuries of A Weekend Warrior

OK, body parts, sound off.
Foot: I can't get a toe-hold today.
Brain: I have a headache.
Arm: Me? A tender tendon.
Nose: I'm running all day long.
Tooth: Put a cap on it, I'm done.
Eyes: Don't like the way I look.
Heart: I don't have any.
Lung: Count me out, I'm breathless.
Liver: Drank too much last night.
Kidney: I'm all flushed out.
Elbow: I'm bent outta shape.
Shoulder: I need a day to cry on myself.
Finger: I can hardly lift it.
Stomach: It aches.
Penis: I can't get up.
Oh, it's gonna be difficult climbin' outta bed.
Think I'll have to go on the Injured Reserve List.

Spring Training Acrostic

S o few phrases
P ermit the soul to
R ise to cerulean skies.
I n the Florida and Arizona sun
N eophytes attempt to impress
G rizzled old coaches with dazzling skills.

T rumpets herald the first pitch.
R ight handers deal from 60 feet away,
A nd on fields around the complex,
I nfielders, outfielders, pitchers and catchers
N ervelessly ask their bodies to
I mitate the exploits of childhood heroes.
N owhere on earth is a better promise made,
G uaranteed to reset the world on its proper orbit.

Swing for The Fences

Writing poetry is
a turn at bat,
a short plate appearance
where you quickly learn
whether you have struck out
or hit for extra bases.
It could be a blast that
has sailed over the fence,
a home run of a poem
that makes you applaud yourself
as you round the bases in joy.
It could be a dribbler
through the infield
which lifts your
poetic average,
but does not represent your best stroke,
and does nothing to connect you to the
cosmic fans sitting in the bleachers.
It could be a strikeout of
a really bad poem,
but it is not the long game of an essay,
or the summer season
of a novel.
So, therefore, I stand,
patiently waiting on deck,
ready to swing for the fences again.

The (Almost) No-Hitter And "The Open Boat"

The Toronto pitcher, one batter away
from a no-hitter, peers in for the sign,
so close to perfection, he can taste it.
How many chances, he wonders,
do I get to go down in baseball history?
In another century, in another story,
a boat, foundering in the waters
off the rugged coastline, fights for survival.
"Why, oh God, do you tease me?" asks the sailor.
The batter sees the pitch, as large as a grapefruit,
and slaps a hard single to right.
"Why, oh God, did you tease me?" asks the pitcher.
There is always hope for the next game, the next trip,
but why must the universe be so cruel
in offering gifts of immortality and life,
only to pull them back with benign vengeance?

The Arc of The Ball

The arc of the ball,
the arc of life—
I could throw a ball then,
watch its trajectory
as it gained height
on its way home to catch
a speeding runner rounding third.
I could pitch then,
mixing fast ball and curve
as I mowed down batters
in Little League games.
Now, sitting in my lawn chair,
behind a wire fence,
I can just watch
the Little League players
who throw the ball with easy abandon.
I get up slowly, creakily, to watch
my grandson advancing to the plate,
and think of the arc of baseballs,
rising majestically to the sky before
plummeting down to the ground.

The Batting Cage

Long ago, in the arcades of Coney Island,
the batting cages beckoned.
You dropped in your quarters,
selected your speed,
and dreamed for the moment,
you were a major leaguer swinging for the fences.
The bat was too heavy, the pitches too fast,
and you flailed with tepid swings,
trying to make contact
with the ball that zipped by
before you saw it.
Now, in the latter innings of my life,
the cage exists as metaphor for
missed chances, and opportunities,
with wild swings hitting nothing but air.
What I'd like is another turn at bat, one
where the sun is shining, the bat feels right,
and I'm twelve again, ready to step up to the plate,
confident this time I'm about to hit it out of the park.

The Losing Pitcher Talks to His Therapist

"Doc, I think I've made a breakthrough.
You made me realize life is more than
pitches thrown, wins and losses.
You supported me in the good times,
when my fastball clipped the corners,
and my curve tied batters up in knots.
You stood by me in the bad times,
when I suffered from performance anxiety
on the mound and in the bedroom.
You made me see I needed the cheers
to validate and enhance my ego,
that I needed the love of the fans
because my mother constantly criticized,
and my father refused to play catch with me.
You opened my eyes to the fact
that my anger at the opposing team
was only lashing out, anger displacement.
You explained my folly of associating
my self-worth with my earned run average.
I am eternally grateful to you,
but I do have a small favor to ask.
Can I see you for an emergency session?
We have a big series coming up."

The Mets Meet the Mets

Wife to husband:
You'll love *La Traviata.*
The opera is lyrical.
Keep your eyes on the main stars.
It's a story of love.
Violetta is in love with Alfredo,
but the course of true love never runs smooth.
It's the best production I've seen in a while.

Husband to Wife:
You'll love the Mets.
The stadium is electric.
Keep your eyes on the main stars.
You gotta love this team.
Wright is batting below .300,
but the baseball gods believe in redemption.
It's the best game I've seen in a while.

He: The singer took too long to die.
She: Will this game ever be over?

The Natural

I am swinging for the fences
in the Class A Poetry League.
Like Roy Hobbs,
I have dropped out of
the major leagues of writing,
and now after ten years away,
I must pack my "Wonder Pen"
to start all over at the bottom.
The wait at the plate seems interminable—
"We'll let you know if it is a hit
six months from now, and then allow you
to run the bases, if published, in a year or so."
Do I have that much time?
I size up each opposing magazine manager
to see what pitches he will call for:
The sensuous curve of a sweet lyric?
The sizzling fastball of blank verse?
The slow change of a long prose/poem?
I brace myself for the inevitable "no,"
dig back in at "we have received."
I must try to spray my writing
to as many fields as possible,
left, center and right, and maybe one day
I will hit a high arc of a towering poem
and bust out all the lights once again.

They Don't Know Punchball

When the national TV baseball announcers
met the word, "punchball," they didn't
even know what it was, thereby denigrating
and obliterating my whole childhood.
It's obvious they never lived in New York.
"Do you punch a baseball with your hand?" they asked.
"No, that would break your hand." Duh.
"What about with a soccer or kickball?"
"No, I don' think that's it."
They looked it up.
"It's like baseball," they said.
"You toss it up to yourself and punch the ball."
How could you guys be so ignorant
of the game that defined my young life?
How could you not know I played
punchball every day in the Second St. Park?
Punchball, are you listening? With a bright, pink
"Spaldeen" tucked into my back pocket.
You jerks can keep your national broadcast.
Just let me go back to my Second Street Park,
and try to hit one out over the tall wire fence.

Third Base Coach

To teach is not to write.
To orchestrate is not to play.
I serve as the third base coach,
waving the true poets towards stardom,
those who have swung and hit
their poems out of the park.
The true pitchers hurl their poems
with marvelous skill and variety.
The true outfielders catch the meaning
of poems landing in their laps.
I serve as the third base coach,
watching the young rookies
come up to the Poetic Major League,
and know by halting step,
the game has passed me by.
Oh, I can still bat out a metaphor,
and rip a wicked line up through the middle,
but realize the tarp has been pulled over me.
Perhaps, it's just a rain delay,
but more probably, the time to walk on home.

Ty Cobb

"Well, son, I'll tell ya since you askin',
the Georgia Peach wasn't, a peach, that is,
kinda more prickly than an ol' cactus plant.
Oh, I'd seen him in his prime,
tearin' up the league, tearin up the bases.
Man, what a thing of beauty—
to see his feet flyin', his spikes gleamin'
in the sun when he stole second.
They say that goodness always
beats the heck outta the devil.
Don't you go believin' that crap.
He was a mean old mister,
old, young, don't matter much which.
He may have been one of the greatest,
up there in almost every category,
but truth is, he weren't right in the head
ever since his father got shot in the head
when the boy was 18, and just called up.
Have sympathy for him, Lord knows,
but take it from me, I'm tellin' ya,
he was angry and crazy his whole life.
Don't be worshiping him none; he ain't
a fittin' choice for your admiration."

Walk-Off Home Run

There's nothing more definitive,
than the home team announcer's call,
"Walk-off home run! Walk off home run,"
assuredly not as famous as Russ Hodges'
"The Giants win the pennant!
The Giants win the pennant,"
but thrilling nonetheless.
In a world of shifting moralities,
and less-than-certain answers,
it is particularly satisfying to see
that the suddenness of a walk-off home run
decides the outcome once and for all.
One knows then with such striking clarity
who has won, who has lost,
that it makes it far easier to face
an unsettling and problematic world.
Let me know where I stand. Do not confuse me
with muddled maybes and puzzling half-truths.
Let me stand in the batter's box,
with the score tied in the bottom of the ninth,
and let me decide with one mighty swing,
and my own free will, whether I win or lose the game.

Whitman Played the Outfield

Mrs. Whitman to her son:
"How come you're always playing baseball?
So much wasted time, Walt.
Why don't you come inside,
and attend to your writing?"
Mrs. Collins to her son:
"How come you're always practicing pitching?
So much wasted time, Billy.
Why don't you come inside,
and write down some of your poems?"
Mrs. Frost to her son:
"How come you're always swinging that bat?
So much wasted time, Robert.
Why don't you come inside,
and decide what you're going to do with your life?"
Maybe more young poets should listen to their mothers,
thus raising the batting average of the arts.
We deem the flight of a long ball more valuable
than feather-light words that soar for centuries
above the far reaches of the upper deck.

End Poems

The Last Out

There is a rhythm to the rain,
a pattern to the seasons.
Beginnings require completions,
and when the last ball was struck –
this time a slow grounder to third,
and a quick throw to first—
we have come full circle once more.
We're relieved at the cessation of tension,
jubilant if our favorite team has won.
Much of life defies expectation;
unforeseen events shake us all,
and uncertainties tax our emotional well-being.
We need the comfort of baseball,
the thwack of the ball into the catcher's glove,
the never varying distance between
the pitcher's mound and the home plate,
the familiarity of the umpire's strike call.
So, when the last out is recorded,
we will collectively breathe a sigh of relief,
secure that the constancy of baseball
will be there again next spring,
awaiting our appeal for cosmic order.

Worshiping Baseball

Emerging from the stands,
I step out of the shadows,
into the sunlight of the open-air cathedral.
I am here to offer devotion to the angels,
not of the left coast, but of those players
who stand at the altar of home plate,
whose mighty blasts seem to touch
the dome of heaven.
I am but a poor acolyte
begging to divine the secrets
of the baseball universe,
the ethereal spark that completes
a 6-4-3 double play,
the lyrical hymn of a curveball
as it circles its way towards home,
the rush of the celestial wind as
the batter fans on three straight pitches.
From my pew, I pray for a ninth-inning hit,
or walk-off home run which will
deliver me into the arms of victory.
But no matter the outcome,
I shall return next week to my church
to sing the praises of the game I worship.

About the Author

Mel Glenn is the author of 12 books for young adults, including *Jump Ball*, *Split Image*, *Who Killed Mr.Chippendale?* which was nominated for the Edgar Allen Poe Mystery Award.

Having retired from the New York City public school system in 2001, after teaching 34 years of high school English, he now devotes his time to reading, writing, and speaking across the country in conferences and schools. His wife, Elyse, also retired after a long career as an elementary school teacher. His son, Jonathan, is a producer of a national news organization, and his son, Andrew, is a software engineer.

Mel Glenn's website is: www.melglenn.com

www.ingramcontent.com/pod-product-compliance
Lightning Source LLC
Chambersburg PA
CBHW071105090426
42737CB00013B/2483